SHABUA DAYS

STUDY GUIDE

Paul Wozniak

CruXPress

Publishing books that matter

Crux Press
5405 Alton Parkway, Suite A-757
Irvine, CA 92604

Crux Press titles may be purchased in bulk for educational, business, or sales promotional uses. For information, please email specialmarkets@cruxpress.com.

Unless otherwise indicated, all Scripture quotations are from the ESV® Bible (The Holy Bible, English Standard Version®), copyright © 2001, 2011, 2016 by Crossway Bibles, a publishing ministry of Good News Publishers. Used by permission. All rights reserved.

Design by Chelsea Wozniak

Printed in the United States of America

ISBN 978-1-949014-01-3 (*Shabua Days Study Guide*)
ISBN 978-1-949014-00-6 (*Shabua Days* Paperback)

CONTENTS

HOW TO USE THIS GUIDE

Often a study guide presents readers with the opportunity to look again at material in the text, be sure they understand the message, and then apply to their lives the truths they have learned. The purpose of this study guide is not to enable you to apply certain principles to your life. Instead, this study guide is designed to help you be sure you understand what you're reading.

This study guide invites you to slow down so that you follow closely the line of thinking, appreciate the examples chosen to support those arguments, and recognize the value of the conclusions presented. Especially at the beginning of the book, you are establishing foundational ideas that will be key to understanding the rest of *Shabua Days* as well as the subsequent books in the series. Then, in later chapters, this study guide will help you more easily understand the significance of the conclusions drawn as well as the thought process that led to them.

You'll also find in each chapter an "I Have a Few Questions" section where you can jot down questions that come to mind as you read... and an "I Want to Remember" spot for you to make notes about facts and ideas you want to remember. If your questions aren't answered by the end of the book, email us at questions@shabua.com. As for those facts and ideas, we hope your collection encourages you to share what you've learned with people who don't know what they don't know about topics like the Big Bang, evolution, and Creation; precedent, pattern, prophecy, and fulfillment; and, of course, *shabua*.

At the back of this book you'll find a leaders guide as well as a detailed table of contents of *Shabua Days*. The leaders guide includes instructions on how to use this study guide in a small-group setting. The detailed contents includes the page numbers of every chapter, heading, section, and figure in the book *Shabua Days*.

Revisiting the material with others in a small-group after you've gone through it for yourself will clarify and reinforce what you're reading. Throughout, the icon **7** next to a question indicates questions you might consider discussing; the icon **S** indicates questions you might look at if time allows. A small group also provides an opportunity for people to ask their questions ("I Have a Few Questions") and share their amazement ("I Want to Remember").

And you are indeed about to embark on a fact-based journey that leads to insights and understandings that will truly amaze.

SESSION 1

Pages 1-26 in *Shabua Days*

The Bible uses shabua to mark past time, present time, and future time. Whether referring to a short, intermediate, or long span of time, the application of shabua is always consistent, predictable, and reliable.

- Shabua Days (page 1)

CHAPTER 1: SHABUA AND BIBLE PRECEDENT, PATTERN, AND PROPHECY

7 THE BIBLE USES SHABUA TO PREDICT FUTURE EVENTS: Why is it important to understand the concept of *shabua*?

THE ORIGIN OF THE SEVEN-DAY WEEK: Why is it significant that the seven-day week appears to have been contrived rather than rooted in a natural phenomenon?

7 NEITHER HIDDEN, NOR IMAGINED, NOR MYSTERIOUS: Why is it important to have the proper perspective when reading Scripture? How does this relate to the optical illusion (Figure 1.1)?

SHABUA

SHABUA IS TRANSLATED "WEEK" OR "SEVEN:" Why is it important to realize that "week" and "seven" do not convey the full and intended meaning of *shabua*?

> *The term shabua means "a complete time period of seven."*

ALTERNATIVE DEFINITIONS AND MEANINGS: Translators work from the same original or Greek text, so why are there so many Bible translations?

LOST IN TRANSLATION: What point about Bible translation in general—and about the translation of the word *shabua* in particular—does the 1965-era black and white tube television set make?

THE ROOT OF THE MATTER: What does the English word *dozen* teach about understanding the Hebrew word *shabua*?

שבע MEANS "SEVEN" AND "COMPLETE:" What more complete meaning of *shabua* than "week" or "seven" do the eight words after *shabua* suggest? What is this root's second primary meaning?

Two primary meanings meld together: Perhaps helped by Figure 1.3—"Strong's usage notes for *shabua*, *shaba*, and *sheba*"—explain what the melding of "seven" and "complete" communicates.

A complete time period of seven: Even when we define *shabua* as "a complete time period of seven," what question needs to be answered when we find the word in Scripture?

Knowing the context is crucial: In light of the preceding question, why is the context of *shabua* crucial? What important fact closes this section? Write it here.

PRECEDENT, PATTERN, AND PROPHECY

KEY WORDS, THEMES, AND CONCEPTS: What do "Momma," "Dada," and 1+1 illustrate about the relationship of precedent and pattern?

BIBLE PRECEDENT: What precedents—key words and fundamental themes and concepts—does the Old Testament book of Genesis introduce? What are some of the New Testament precedents introduced in Matthew, Mark, Luke, and John?

Consider an artist who sketches his entire design on canvas with graphite pencil before beginning to paint. The Old Testament can be compared to that detailed sketch. Although the drawing may be beautiful, the artist never intended the work to be complete without color. The New Testament picks up where the Old Testament leaves off by adding vibrant color. Just as it is not essential to have seen the artist's initial sketch to appreciate the finished painting, it is not essential to know the Old Testament to understand the basic message of the New Testament.

7 BIBLE PATTERNS BASED ON BIBLE PRECEDENT: What does the artist's example illustrate about the relationship between the Old Testament and the New Testament?

S THE OLD TESTAMENT IS 77% OF THE BIBLE: Too many churches neglect the Old Testament because, in part, we can appreciate the finished painting (the New Testament) without having seen the artist's sketch (the Old Testament). What attitude toward the Old Testament do you have? What has previously been communicated to you about the value of the Old Testament?

> *Precedents and patterns initiated in the Old Testament are often completed in the New Testament as the fulfillment of Bible prophecy, and the value of our knowing the significance and relevance of that fact cannot be overstated.*

PROPHECY IS A PREDICTION OF FUTURE EVENTS: Like students who only know math-by-calculator—do you only know the Christian faith in terms of the New Testament? Whatever your answer, what was your initial response to the statement "New Testament readers don't know what they don't know"?

AN EXAMPLE IN THE SACRIFICIAL SYSTEM: Summarize the sacrificial system and how it exemplifies an Old Testament precedent and pattern reaching its prophetic fulfillment in the New Testament.

S FROM PRECEDENT... TO PATTERN... TO PROPHECY: Why are the terms in Figure 1.4—"Precedent, pattern, and prophecy"—introduced in this discussion of *shabua*-days?

A PREVIEW OF COMING ATTRACTIONS: Figure 1.5—"Topics covered in *Shabua Days*"—outlines the book. Which of the coming chapters do you most look forward to reading? Why?

Write or list one or two takeaways from chapter 1 that you found most eye-opening, helpful, and/or intriguing.

> *There are two distinct worldviews: the biblical and the secular. The biblical worldview is based on the account of Creation (the beginning of the universe and the diversity of living things). The secular worldview is based on the theories of the Big Bang (the beginning of the universe) and evolution (the diversity of living things).*

CHAPTER 2: CREATION, THE BIG BANG, AND EVOLUTION

7 Two DISTINCT WORLDVIEWS: Which worldview do you currently adhere to, the biblical or the secular? Why?

THE INAUGURAL SHABUA

S WHETHER IN MILLISECONDS OF TRILLIONS OF YEARS...: If *God created*, the length of time He took to create pales in significance next to the very fact that God *did* create. But the length of time does matter. Why? Give two or three reasons.

S VARIOUS INTERPRETATIONS OF A BIBLICAL DAY: People generally believe that the interpretation of *day* in Genesis 1 is up for discussion. Review the questions on page 20 of *Shabua Days*. Which points had you not considered? In light of your understanding of Creation, which argument do you find the most convincing?

A DAY IS A PERIOD OF DARKNESS AND LIGHT: What basic fact about the length of a day does Genesis 1:3-5 establish? Why is that important?

EACH DAY ENDS THE SAME WAY: Why do the people living in Israel recognize sunset as simultaneously the end and the beginning of very 24-hour day?

CONNECTIONS TO A 24-HOUR DAY: Explain in your own words how Exodus 20:8 supports the argument that day in Genesis 1 refers to a 24-hour period.

BOOKENDS OF CREATION: What is a natural, logical, and reasonable explanation for the continuing supply of living things on planet Earth? And why is that explanation relevant in this chapter's discussion of Creation and evolution?

JESUS WAS PRESENT AT CREATION: Why is Jesus' presence at Creation significant to this discussion of *day*?

JESUS AND THE BEGINNING: Do you agree that the Genesis 1:1 and Matthew 19:4 words *the beginning* do not appear to be at all figurative or subjective? Why or why not?

7 No new creation until the eternal state: Explain why the statement *the heavens and the earth were finished* (Genesis 2:1) is significant in the argument of the Big Bang and evolution.

The 7th and final day of the shabua: In the Bible, *shabua* is a term that refers to "a complete time period of seven" with the 7th interval being different from the preceding six. What was different about the 7th day in Genesis 1?

Shabath describes the action of resting: Emphasizing its importance, *shabath* appears twice in reference to what God did on the 7th and final day of the inaugural *shabua*. What is the double meaning of *shabath*?

God chose the 7th and final day of the first shabua to both cease and rest from the work of creating. Six intervals of work followed by a 7th and final interval of rest establish a biblical shabua.

S THE INAUGURAL SHABUA IS SHABUA-DAYS: At this point, what would you say to a person wanting the Genesis 1 use of *day* to mean something other than a 24-hour period?

CREATION OR THE BIG BANG?: Creation cannot be proved because it cannot be replicated and nobody saw it happen. On the other hand, there is no way to disprove it. Likewise, the theory of the Big Bang—the alternative to biblical Creation—cannot be proved because it cannot be replicated and nobody saw it happen, yet—again—there is no way to disprove it. Why, then, do most people prefer the Big Bang theory?

Whether you are inclined to believe in Creation or the Big Bang... you will see that the differences between these two mutually exclusive views are so great they cannot be reconciled. In other words, both cannot be true.

I Want to Remember

I Have a Few Questions

SESSION 2

Pages 26-56 in *Shabua Days*

The inaugural shabua incorporates the biblical account of Creation. Creation is the biblical view of the beginning of everything.

\- Shabua Days (page 17)

CHAPTER 2: CREATION, THE BIG BANG, AND EVOLUTION

THE BIG BANG'S UNIVERSE

THE SUN, THE STARS, AND THE MILKY WAY GALAXY: What do you make of the fact that estimates as to the number of stars in the Milky Way Galaxy range from 100 billion to 400 billion to maybe a trillion? Also, to what do you attribute the wide range? Why is there such uncertainty?

S GALAXIES AND THE HUBBLE SPACE TELESCOPE: Estimates about the number of galaxies in the universe also range widely from 200 billion to 2 trillion. Why is it significant that, with each advance in technology, the numbers always seem to increase rather than decrease?

HUBBLE DEEP FIELDS: Knowledge has increased as technology has improved. Compare the different numbers of galaxies found in the three HST surveys (page 27-28 in *Shabua Days*). Why are findings like these significant in a discussion of Creation and the Big Bang?

A light-second is the distance that light travels in one second, which is 299,792 kilometers (186,282 miles)... A light-year is the distance that light travels in one year, which is 9.5 trillion kilometers (5.9 trillion miles).

MEASURING DISTANCES AT LIGHT SPEED: Proxima Centauri, the closest star to Earth, is still 4.2 light-years away, and the Andromeda Galaxy, the closest galaxy to our Milky Way Galaxy, is a staggering 2.5 million light-years away. What is your intellectual, emotional, and spiritual response to these truly unfathomable numbers?

ERASMUS DARWIN'S EXPLOSIVE BEGINNING: What was your initial reaction to the fact that the Big Bang theory originated as an abstract idea in a 1791 poem by Erasmus Darwin (Charles Darwin's grandfather)?

THE "PRIMORDIAL PARTICLE" OF EDGAR ALLEN POE: Probably influenced by Erasmus Darwin, the American writer Edgar Allen Poe proposed that the universe began when a single "primordial Particle" fragmented, and the particles spread out in all directions from a center. One characteristic of this particle, Poe continued, is its "infinite divisibility." What would you say to either counter or support the idea of infinite divisibility? Be as scientific or nonscientific as you want.

ALEKSANDR FRIEDMANN AND GEORGES LEMAÎTRE: Using mathematics, what did Friedmann and, later, Lemaître learn about the universe? What do you think was the response of their fellow scientists of the early twentieth century? Why?

ASTRONOMER EDWIN HUBBLE AND HUBBLE'S LAW: What did astronomer Edwin Hubble prove in 1929?

To picture an expanding universe——the essence of Hubble's Law——mark a deflated balloon with dots to represent galaxies. When the balloon is inflated, each dot is uniformly spread out or stretched out at a rate that is proportional to the distance from the center and each other.
"Take a minute to do the balloon demonstration if you haven't already.

REDSHIFTS PROVE THE UNIVERSE IS EXPANDING: Why do we refer to the phenomenon of the universe expanding as Hubble's Law rather than Hubble's Theory?

LEMAÎTRE'S INITIAL QUANTUM AND PRIMEVAL ATOM: Having confirmed that the universe is expanding, why might Lemaître propose the existence of a "primeval atom"?

A COSMIC CATACLYSM CALLED THE BIG BANG: Look again at National Geographic's description of the Big Bang. What details, if any, do you feel exceed credibility?

S A SINGULARITY OF INFINITE DENSITY: What was your reaction to the statement that a singularity can "[cause] the rules that govern matter to break down"? Is it significant or concerning that the laws of physics can be broken? What would you say to a scientist dismissing the Big Bang's broken law of physics as a onetime event?

THE ORIGIN OF THE SINGULARITY IS AN ENIGMA: What questions does the supposed existence of a singularity raise? What are some of the various responses from the scientific community?

THE SIZE OF THE SOLAR SYSTEM IN .00001 SECONDS: Again, what details, if any, in this section and especially in the National Geographic excerpt weaken the credibility of the Big Bang theory?

How did we go from a fact that has scientifically been proven true——the universe is expanding——to the inference that the universe was once an extremely small particle?

S THE ACCELERATING RATE OF UNIVERSE EXPANSION: How did scientists come to the conclusion that the Earth is 13.8 billion years old? What do other scientists say in rebuttal?

NEWTON'S FIRST AND SECOND LAWS OF MOTION: Astronomers have observed distant galaxies moving away from Earth at an increasing velocity. What commentary do the First and Second Laws of Motion offer? What is "dark energy"? Why do scientists talk about "dark energy"?

ONLY ONE POINT OF VIEW IS PRESENTED: Reflect on your school years. What conclusion(s) do you remember drawing about the origin of everything? If evolution, the Big Bang, and/or the biblical Creation account were taught, what were your impressions about the validity of the ideas presented?

THE DEFINITION OF A SCIENTIFIC THEORY: Why might scientists struggle to agree on the definition of scientific theory?

"LOGICAL, TESTABLE, AND PREDICTIVE": So how well do the two key components of the Big Bang theory—an expanding universe and a singularity—meet the criteria of logical? testable? predictive? What is your opinion about the singularity? Does it qualify as a valid theory?

THE LARGE HADRON COLLIDER: What is the sophisticated LHC trying to simulate and therefore to prove?

THE LHC DOES NOT TEST THE INITIAL BIG BANG: Comment on the value and purpose of the LHC when it isn't testing some monumental issues that are at the heart of the Big Bang. What statement(s) in this section did you find surprising?

7 PHASES OF THE UNIVERSE AFTER THE BIG BANG: The properties and composition of the singularity cannot be explained or tested, and scientists do not address the issue of its origin. What happens to the Big Bang theory if the existence of a singularity is dismissed? Why do you think the singularity remains the leading explanation for an entire universe of energy, matter, space, and time?

The properties and composition of the singularity cannot be explained or tested, and scientists do not address the issue of its origin. Nevertheless, the singularity is the leading explanation for an entire universe of energy, matter, space, and time. Without the singularity, the Big Bang does not bang, and all subsequent assumptions about the universe are called into question.

S FAITH IN THE BIG BANG OR CREATION: Faith is the choice to believe in something that can't be proved. What are supporters of the Big Bang theory putting their faith in?

THE BIBLE'S UNIVERSE

THE INAUGURAL SHABUA-DAYS: Summarize the inaugural *shabua*-days described in Genesis 1 and 2. Then we'll look more closely at certain elements of that precedent-setting week.

> *It might help to consider the materials God created on Day 1 as equivalent to a six-day supply of water and clay that a potter would procure before getting to work. Just as a potter molds and shapes beautiful pots using these raw materials, God molded and shaped His creation—over a period of six days—primarily from the elements He made on Day 1.*

7 "IN THE BEGINNING, GOD CREATED": Genesis 1:1-3 describes an activity that no human being has experienced. What does the potter analogy help clarify?

7 DAY 1: What three elements did God create on Day 1 and then use in the creative work that followed? Why is the phrase "in their most elementary form" fundamental to the creation account as a whole?

DAY 2: What is the connection between what God created on Day 1 and what He created on Day 2?

DAY 3: What is the connection between what God created on Day 1 and what He created on Day 3?

DAY 4: What is the connection between what God created on Day 1 and what He created on Day 4? Look at Figures 2.5, 2.6, 2.7, 2.8 and note the progression.

> *The universe ("what is seen") was created when God literally spoke it ("by the word of God") into existence from something that human beings are not able to see ("not made out of things that are visible").*

GOD CREATED THE UNIVERSE WITH HIS WORD: The Bible teaches that God didn't speak the universe into existence until Day 4. Why does this time frame explain the existence of ice on comets, asteroids, and planets?

THE EPICENTER OF THE UNIVERSE: The point where the hypothetical singularity exploded would be the epicenter of the universe, but astrophysicists have not been able to identify that spot. Why do you think they won't even consider the possibility that Earth is in the vicinity of the epicenter?

THE FOUNDATION OF THE EARTH: What details in the Creation account support the possibility that Earth—first nebulous and then created—is the foundation for everything else that God created?

GOD STRETCHED/SPREAD OUT THE UNIVERSE: What support that Earth is the epicenter of the universe does Isaiah 40:22 offer?

GOD FORMED EARTH BEFORE THE UNIVERSE: We read in Genesis that God formed planet Earth on Day 3, and He formed the universe on Day 4. In what ways does this account contradict the Big Bang theory?

The sequence of what was created when is highly significant.

STRETCHED OUT LIKE A CURTAIN, SPREAD LIKE A TENT: What does the curtain metaphor help you better understand about Hubble's Law? How does this metaphor support the possibility that Earth is the epicenter of the universe?

The Bible's universe cannot be reconciled with the Big Bang's universe. The two views completely contradict each other in regard to both the order and the timing.

7 The two views cannot be reconciled: What are some of the ways that the Creation account and modern science are in sync? Why is that Bible-science correlation important to some people?

7 The sequence and timing differ: Figure 2.14 compares the biblical worldview of the sequence and timing to the secular worldview. What do you notice about each separately? What stands out as you compare the two?

I Want to Remember

I Have a Few Questions

SESSION 3

Pages 57-87 in *Shabua Days*

From the smallest subatomic particles to a fully functioning human body, we find exquisite order, microscopic detail, and meticulous design. The relevant question is not whether order, detail, and design exist——we ourselves are evidence that they do——but how did this happen?

- Shabua Days (page 75)

CHAPTER 2: CREATION, THE BIG BANG, AND EVOLUTION

EVOLUTION'S DIVERSITY

ERASMUS DARWIN'S HYPOTHESIS OF EVOLUTION: What was Erasmus Darwin's contribution to the hypothesis of evolution? What did his grandson Charles Darwin contribute to the discussion?

THE PROGRESSION OF CHARLES DARWIN'S THEORIES: Charles Darwin believed that the native inhabitants of Fuego had not yet completed the transition from wild animals to domesticated human beings. What is a more realistic explanation of the differences Charles saw between the people of Fuego and the people of England? Why might Charles have chosen his explanation?

CHARLES DARWIN'S ON THE ORIGIN OF SPECIES: In what two ways and to what two audiences did Darwin get his ideas out? What resulted from this two-prong approach?

Encyclopædia Britannica says that evolution is a "theory in biology postulating that the various types of plants, animals, and other living things on Earth have their origin in other preexisting types and that the distinguishable differences are due to modifications in successive generations."

THE THEORY OF EVOLUTION: What are your thoughts about "the central idea of biological evolution is that all life on Earth shares a common ancestor"?

S THE BIG BANG, EVOLUTION, AND A PROKARYOTE: The theory of evolution proposes a process to explain the diversity of life on planet Earth. First, what is the prokaryote? Second, what critical aspect of the origin of life—of the prokaryote—do both the Big Bang and evolution fail to address?

THE SOLAR SYSTEM, SUN, PLANETS, AND EARTH: What evolutionary stage is illustrated by the image of a spinning CD or DVD collapsing into its hollow center to form a small plastic marble? What basic force is arguably key to the increasing size of Earth during the creation phase of its existence?

EARTH WAS AND STILL IS A MOLTEN FIREBALL: In comparing Earth to an egg, what is Earth's yolk? What detail, if any, do you find striking in this discussion?

The surface of Earth is approximately 71% water and 29% dry land.

332,519,000 CUBIC MILES OF WATER ON EARTH: What percentage of Earth's surface would you have estimated was water? Does the actual statistic surprise you? Why or why not?

WATER ON EARTH FROM ICE IN COMETS: What are three arguments against the idea that the planet's 332,519,000 cubic miles of water came from ice in comets that melted after impacting Earth? What would you say in rebuttal to any or all three?

S THE SOURCE OF EARTH'S WATER IS UNRESOLVED: Why is *how* and *when* water appeared on Earth relevant to the origin of life? Explain.

SEVEN THEORIES ON THE ORIGIN OF LIFE: Review the seven theories on the origin of life (pages 64-65). What do some of the theories require advocates to put their faith in?

THE ORIGIN OF LIFE IS UNRESOLVED: Explain how the Panspermia theory deflects the question of how life began. The Big Bang theory and the theory of evolution also fail to address the origin of life. What does each focus on instead?

EVOLUTION ADDRESSES DIVERSITY, NOT ORIGIN: Evolution is presented as proven fact. If evolution did occur, what kinds of supporting evidence would be available to scientists—but isn't?

1 GRAM OF DNA = 1,000,000,000 TERABYTES: What account of the origin of life and/or the diversity of life is supported by the incredible complexity of life? Explain.

PROBABILITY IS A MEASURE OF THE ODDS: What does the monkey sitting at the keyboard suggest about the possible evolution of DNA with its 1 billion terabytes of data?

THE SECOND LAW OF THERMODYNAMICS AND ENTROPY: What is the Second Law of Thermodynamics—and how does it contradict the theory of evolution?

Throughout the universe both impeccable order and meticulous design are found everywhere and in everything.

S IMPECCABLE ORDER AND METICULOUS DESIGN: Would people believe someone who said a copper penny formed itself from the ore as a result of natural processes? Why or why not? Why do some people believe that a goldfish or a golden retriever formed itself from the necessary preexisting ingredients as a result of natural processes? Explain.

A PROKARYOTE'S DESIGN IS INTRICATE AND COMPLEX: Would you believe someone who said energy and matter (nonliving) became a prokaryote (living) through natural processes? Why or why not?

A fully functioning human body requires an integrated network of body systems all working simultaneously, and each body system further requires multiple organs and tissues all working simultaneously. If one single tissue or organ is not functioning properly, a body system is affected; and if one single body system is not functioning properly, the entire body is affected.

HUMAN BODY SYSTEMS, ORGANS, AND TISSUES: What facts about the human body suggest there is nothing random about its existence?

THE EYE HAS THIRTEEN ANCILLARY PARTS: What was your initial response to this section and its rhetorical questions? Would these facts cause evolutionists to pause and consider an alternative explanation to life on this planet? Why or why not?

THE MALE AND FEMALE REPRODUCTIVE SYSTEMS: In response to this presentation of the complexity of reproduction for human beings and chickens, what might evolutionists say in defense of their viewpoint?

DEVELOPMENT AND DIVISION OF THE SEXES: The sexes evolved together and split. The sexes evolved independently but found each other and discovered their complementary parts. What would be yet another possibility to the origin of the sexes?

CELLS, DNA, AND NUCLEOTIDES: What fact about DNA did you find most remarkable? Take time to marvel.

ATOMS, PROTONS, NEUTRONS, ELECTRONS, QUARKS, AND LEPTONS: What might evolutionists say about these particles of matter? How might they fit the existence of atoms, protons, neutrons, electrons, quarks, and leptons into their theory?

RANDOM TRANSITIONS INCREASING IN COMPLEXITY: Review the list of supposedly random transitions that eventually resulted in human beings (pages 75-76). Which is harder to believe—this series of events or the existence of a Creator God? Why do some people reject Creator God?

THE HUMAN MIND IS A MYSTERY: Why is it significant that evolution cannot explain the *how* or the *why* of the human mind or emotions?

THE BIBLE'S DIVERSITY

S LIVING THINGS CAME FROM EARTH'S SOIL: What remarkable alignment between the Bible and science is presented here? Take time to read "Building Blocks of Life" if you haven't.

"ACCORDING TO THEIR KINDS": What is the Bible's explanation for the existence of the sexes and their complementary reproductive systems?

7 CREATED MATURE WITH THE ABILITY TO REPRODUCE: Explain why it is safe to infer that God created mature versions of everything that He created.

IF NOT CREATED MATURE, THEN WHAT?: Why is it only natural, logical, and reasonable to conclude that God created a mature Adam and a mature Eve?

Each initial created kind (family/genus) contained a comprehensive genome that enabled it to produce every type (species) within its own kind.

EACH KIND CONTAINED A COMPREHENSIVE GENOME: The Bible's *kind* and the Bible's *type* correspond in the same way that our words *family/genus* and *species* do. What is significant about the fact that God created all living things to be fruitful and multiply "according to their own kinds"?

S HUMAN BEINGS ARE A CREATED KIND: What is noteworthy about the 0.1% variation in human DNA?

THE ARK AT THE TIME OF THE FLOOD: In light of the fact that Noah's three-deck ark was 1.5 football fields long, why is it significant that God commanded him to bring a pair of each *kind* on board, not every *type*?

> *The identical terminology used to describe God's creation of kinds in Genesis 1 is used to describe God's preservation of kinds at the time of the flood in Genesis 6.*

KINDS AT THE TIME OF THE FLOOD: In Hebrew literature repetition indicates emphasis. What phrase is repeated in Genesis 6:20, and why would it be emphasized?

LIVING THINGS ARE DIVERSE AND SIMILAR: What two aspects of the creation account are replicated every moment of every day? In what way are all living things—a rose bush, a scorpion, a blue whale, and a human being—similar?

The Bible's kinds (God-created diversity) cannot be reconciled with the theory of evolution (serendipity-created diversity).

7 THE BIBLE'S KINDS VS. EVOLUTION: The Bible's kinds (God-created diversity) and evolution (serendipity-created diversity) cannot be reconciled. What does the biblical account address that evolution skips over, and why is that skipping over significant?

7 THE REASON EVOLUTION IS SO DOMINANT: Why is evolution the dominant understanding of how the diversity of living things came to be? Name one or two unresolved issues, any of which would cast doubt on the entire theory.

THE BIBLE VS. SECULAR SCIENCE

7 TODAY'S WORLDVIEW IS INCOMPATIBLE WITH THE BIBLE: The Big Bang with its exploding singularity and evolution with the development of all living things from a primitive single-celled microorganism is incompatible with the Bible account. So why do some people try to, for instance, align the Big Bang theory with Genesis 1?

Despite the overwhelming conflicts between the Bible and secular science, these different perspectives have one aspect in common. Belief in Creation, belief in the Big Bang, and belief in evolution all require faith.

FAITH IN SOMEONE, SOMETHING, OR A PROCESS: Whichever account of creation we accept, we are putting our faith in *Someone*, in *something*, or in a *process*. Are you placing your faith in God as Creator, in the explosion of a singularity, or in the process of evolution? Why? Or maybe you're not yet ready to put your faith in Someone, in something, or in a process. Write down your questions and reservations—and find someone to talk to about them.

7 SHABUA-DAYS HAVE A MEANING AND PURPOSE: What would your simple answer be if someone asked you, "What are *shabua*-days?" Also, what are three purposes of *shabua*-days?

THE WORD OF GOD HAS BEEN PRESERVED: Do you agree that if God did in fact create all that exists, the length of time it took Him to create may seem of secondary importance and perhaps even irrelevant. As we'll see, the *shabua*-days precedent that we see in the Creation account is significant. What reasons are mentioned here?

Write or list one or two takeaways from chapter 2 that you found most eye-opening, helpful, and/or intriguing.

I Want to Remember

I Have a Few Questions

SESSION 4

Pages 89-118 in *Shabua Days*

Sabbath means "rest," and it is the title for the 7th and final interval of a shabua, which is a complete time period of seven.

- Shabua Days (page 109)

CHAPTER 3: A BIBLICAL WEDDING, MANNA, AND THE FOURTH COMMANDMENT

A BIBLICAL WEDDING

ABRAHAM, ISAAC, AND JACOB: According to the corresponding verses, why is each new name appropriate? (Remember Jacob's story.)

Abraham: Genesis 17:5; 22:17-18

Jacob: Genesis 25:31-33; Genesis 27:19-30

Israel: Genesis 32:24 -28

JACOB SERVED SEVEN YEARS FOR RACHEL: What happened to the supplanter and schemer in this situation?

7 COMPLETE THE WEEK = COMPLETE THE SHABUA: Why will references to *shabua*-days help align biblical accounts with other historical records?

S A BIBLICAL WEDDING IS A SHABUA: Why is it significant that we see a second *shabua* in Scripture?

> *A biblical wedding is a complete time period of seven days, and it incorporates each distinct element of a shabua.*

MANNA

JACOB AND HIS 69 DESCENDANTS: Behind the statement that three of Jacob's sons were already in Egypt is the amazing life story of Joseph, Jacob's favorite. Genesis 37-45 makes for a good read. God's sovereign hand in preserving his chosen people is remarkable and wonderful. In what ways have you seen the sovereign hand of God in your life?

GOD REMEMBERED HIS COVENANT: What aspect of this ancient story—or characteristic of God—encourages you today in the twenty-first century?

Blood from the basin was applied—with a hyssop branch—to the doorframe's horizontal top beam (the lintel) as well as to the right and left vertical side supports (the doorposts)... The four areas in the doorway marked in blood form a cross pattern.

THE ISRAELITES WERE PASSED OVER: What is a new-to-you or a favorite fact from this discussion of the first Passover?

7 THE EXODUS FROM EGYPT: Identify the precedent and the pattern discussed in this section and the previous one. You may even know the prophetic aspect of Passover. If so, please share it.

30 DAYS AFTER LEAVING EGYPT: What very human trait did the Israelites display—and what essential traits of God did they then see?

40 YEARS OF BREAD FROM HEAVEN: Review the details. What are some of God's traits—in addition to what you may have mentioned in response to the previous question—revealed in this section?

AN OMER OF MANNA EACH DAY: What do the remarkable traits of manna reveal about the nature of God the Father?

MANNA IN PRECEDENT, PATTERN, AND PROPHECY: Summarize how manna in the wilderness foreshadowed both the coming and the mission of Jesus.

A DOUBLE PORTION ON THE SIXTH DAY: What two events does the double-portion-on-the-sixth-day refer to? And what do you notice about God in this precedent/pattern?

7 SHABUA-DAYS OF MANNA: What precedent established in the *shabua*-days of Creation is repeated in the *shabua*-days of manna?

THE 7TH AND FINAL DAY IS THE SABBATH: What Hebrew name is given to the 7th and final day of the *shabua*—and what is its English translation?

SHABBATH AND SHABATH HAVE SIMILAR MEANINGS: *Shabbath* and *shabath* have similar meanings. What does *shabath* mean in Genesis, and what does *Shabbath* mean in Exodus?

> *Consider a father who desires to bless his son with a gift. If the son does not accept the gift, he will not receive the benefits his father intended, and the gift will be meaningless. Similarly, the Israelites needed to accept their heavenly Father's gift of the Sabbath. They did so by ceasing from work and resting on the 7th and final day of every shabua.*

THE SABBATH IS GOD'S GIFT OF REST TO ISRAEL: Why is it significant that the Sabbath is a gift, not merely a command?

THE FOURTH COMMANDMENT

THE FOURTH COMMANDMENT FORMALIZED THE SABBATH: Why does it make sense that God expanded the definition of work beyond gathering manna?

S A NATURAL, LOGICAL, AND REASONABLE CONCLUSION: Do you agree that the Fourth Commandment pattern supports the argument that each day of Creation is a 24-hour period? Is that "the most natural, logical, and reasonable interpretation"? Why or why not?

A SIGN FOREVER BETWEEN GOD AND ISRAEL: Why did God command the people of Israel to observe the Sabbath?

THE SABBATH IS FUNDAMENTAL TO JUDAISM: In your opinion, why do Jews today faithfully observe the Sabbath? Consider that they don't live under a covenant of grace. Also comment on the Muslim practice of Jumu'ah: what, if anything, do you make of its similarities to the Jews' Sabbath?

Shabua-days and the Sabbath are unique aspects of God's relationship with the "people of Israel."

7 CHRISTIAN OPINIONS REGARDING THE SABBATH: If you are a Christian, what has been your general attitude toward the Sabbath? Why?

REST ON THE SABBATH VS. MEETING ON SUNDAY: Why do Christians choose to gather for worship on Sunday (the first day of the week) rather than Saturday (the 7th and final day of a *shabua*)?

S TWO ADDITIONAL REFERENCES TO SUNDAY: Why might it be significant that not a single verse or passage in the entire Bible commands believers to either meet or rest on Sunday?

GATHERING IS NOT A SUBSTITUTE FOR REST: What impact did the Israelites' exile to Babylon have on their practice of their faith during that time and even after?

THE HEBREW WORD FOR SABBATH: The same Hebrew root is incorporated in six Hebrew words. What concept is therefore embedded in the meaning of those words?

THE TWO PRIMARY MEANINGS OF SABBATH: What are the two primary meanings of Sabbath, and what connection between those two meanings do you see?

CONSEQUENCES FOR VIOLATING THE SABBATH: For whom is the Sabbath not a suggestion or option? What events in Israel's history showed the value God places on their obeying the Fourth Commandment?

THE EXTRABIBLICAL SABBATH LAWS OF THE PHARISEES: What is the upside— the noble intention—of these laws? What are some downsides?

JESUS OUTRAGED THE PHARISEES ON THE SABBATH: According to the beginning of the second paragraph in this section, what had the Sabbath become? What explicit actions of Jesus bothered the Jews—and what message about His identity was implied by those actions?

In addition to the rest that Jesus provides for the mind and body, Jesus offers spiritual rest for the soul. That kind of rest happens when a believer comes under the yoke of Jesus and learns how to cope with the burdens of life by following His way.

7 JESUS IS THE PROPHETIC FULFILLMENT OF REST: Why can we be sure that Jesus never violated the Sabbath—and what does that fact suggest about the Pharisees' laws and why Jesus' actions upset them?

All burdens are not eliminated when believers take up the yoke that Jesus offers, but the burdens do become—as Jesus promised—easier and lighter, and in the process believers do find rest for their souls.

S JESUS USES THE METAPHOR OF A YOKE FOR REST: What kind of rest does Jesus offer—and how is that different from the Old Testament rest commanded in the Fourth Commandment? Also, describe what Christians see as significant about the structure of the farmer's yoke that Jesus invites His followers to metaphorically take on.

JESUS OFFERS REST ANY DAY, ANYTIME, ANYPLACE: Explain the connection between finding rest in Jesus, abiding in Him, and gathering in community with His people.

THE ONE COMMANDMENT NOT EXPRESSLY RESTATED: Had you ever noticed that the Fourth Commandment is the only one of the ten that is not expressly restated in the New Testament? Why might that be? In chapter 5 you'll find a detailed analysis.

THE SABBATH IS GOD'S COVENANT WITH ISRAEL: Jesus did not extend the Fourth Commandment to the Gentile church, nor did He expand its meaning to include mind and heart. What reason for His silence about this matter do you find here?

SABBATH PRECEDENT, PATTERN, AND PROPHECY: Identify the precedent... the pattern... and the way the prophecy was fulfilled.

Believers can go to Jesus to find rest at any time, on any day, and from any location on planet Earth. The rest that Jesus provides is not limited to Sunday, the Sabbath, or a church building.

GOD'S COMMANDMENT TO THE JEWS: What two groups of Jews continue to observe the Sabbath by resting on Saturday?

CONCLUDING SUMMARY: After reviewing this summary section, look again at the four bulleted points in the preceding section. Do you agree/disagree with each of those conclusions? Why?

Write or list one or two takeaways from chapter 3 that you found most eye-opening, helpful, and/or intriguing.

I Want to Remember

I Have a Few Questions

SESSION 5

Pages 119-136 in *Shabua Days*

An individual who takes the time to diligently study the Old Testament feasts will be rewarded with a much greater understanding and appreciation of their New Testament prophetic fulfillment evident in Jesus' life and the birth of the church.

- Shabua Days (page 126)

CHAPTER 4: THE SEVEN-DAY FEAST

THREE PRIMARY BIBLICAL FEASTS

7 MANY BIBLICAL CORRELATIONS HAVE BEEN LOST: Why is the interrelationship between the Old Testament, the New Testament, and the biblical feasts not obvious in the twenty-first century?

EACH FEAST IS ASSOCIATED WITH A CROP: What did faithful Jewish men do in observance of the three primary biblical feasts?

The Bible refers to the first portion of a crop that is harvested for a special ceremony as firstfruits. In this ceremony, the people presented to God the firstfruits of the crop before beginning the actual work of harvesting the fields.

7 FIRSTFRUITS OF BARLEY AND WHEAT: What were the people of Israel proclaiming when they gave God the first portion of the crop?

THE FRUIT OF THE VINE: List some facts that support the conclusion that Jesus drank pure, fresh grape juice during the Last Supper.

SYMBOLISM IN THE THREE FEASTS: What did/does each of the Old Testament feasts point to?

Feast of Passover

Feast of *Shabua*

Feast of Ingathering

7 FEASTS IN PRECEDENT, PATTERN, AND PROPHECY: What teachings do Orthodox Jews appreciate—and what do they have little, if any, understanding of? And what teachings do Christians greatly appreciate—and what do they have little, if any, understanding of? If you fall into one of those categories, is the statement true about you? Comment on why that is the case.

THE EDICT OF MILAN IN 313 CE: What significant change did Emperor Constantine make with his Edict of Milan? List both pros and cons of that change in governmental policy.

THE MEETING OF THE COUNCIL OF NICAEA IN 325 CE: What religious decision was the Council of Nicaea responsible for? What was lost with this change?

S FEASTS ARE A SHADOW OF THINGS TO COME: Note some negative aspects of the decree of the Council of Nicaea. Be sure to discuss the impact of the opinion that the Gentile church had replaced Israel.

MARKING TIME IN THE BIBLE

S BEFORE CALENDARS, CELL PHONES, CLOCKS, COMPUTERS...: Why is it important to remember details about the very different world of Bible times?

> *The Bible uses the sun to mark days, shabua-days to mark weeks, the moon to mark months, and the agricultural seasons and farming cycle to mark years.*

7 FARMING CYCLE AND AGRICULTURAL SEASONS: Why was the farming cycle used to mark years in Bible times—and what are the components of a farming cycle?

THE BIBLICAL YEAR AND THE TRADITIONAL YEAR: Who changed the beginning of the biblical year to Nisan? What role did the month of Tishri continue to play in Jewish life?

THE BIBLE CITES SPECIFIC DATES: The annual agricultural seasons were used to determine each biblical year. Why did the people of Israel need more precise timekeeping?

The Bible cites the specific dates—such as the fifteenth day of the first month—on which feasts, festivals, and holy days are to be celebrated, and people were required to know exactly when that was.

THE MOON MARKS MONTHS AND SEASONS: In addition to obeying God, why is it important for Jewish feasts to be celebrated when God specifies?

THE FIRST SIGHTING OF THE NEW MOON AT SUNSET: The first sighting of the new moon at sunset marked the first day of each biblical month. Why was this method chosen? Give two or three reasons.

ROSH CHODESH IS THE NEW MOON FESTIVAL: What kind of confirmation of the new moon was required?

THE PHASES OF THE MOON: The Bible's term new moon means something different from the modern usage of new moon. What is the difference, and why is that difference important for us to know as we study Scripture?

29-DAY AND 30-DAY BIBLICAL MONTHS: A lunar month lasts 29.5 days. What did the Hebrews do with that half-day as they established biblical months?

S SYNCHRONIZING THE LUNAR AND SOLAR YEARS: What did the Sanhedrin do to synchronize biblical months (the lunar cycle) to their respective agricultural seasons (the solar cycle)? Why did the Jews need this synchronization?

S RABBI HILLEL INTRODUCED A FIXED CALENDAR: Orthodox Jews use this nineteen-year cyclical formula Rabbi Hillel created. Why is it significant that this method is not found in the Bible?

7 SCIENTIFIC DATING AND ASTRONOMICAL EVENTS: Of what value is this effort to pinpoint biblical events?

God has given our generation of believers a precious gift: we have the ability to scientifically confirm the accuracy of the Bible.

I Want to Remember

I Have a Few Questions

SESSION 6

Pages 136-170 in *Shabua Days*

The initial sacrifice of lambs in Egypt (precedent), the ritual sacrifice of lambs on the first day of the Seven-Day Feast (pattern), and the sacrifice of Jesus——the Lamb of God——on a cross in Jerusalem (prophecy) all occurred on the exact same date: Nisan 14.

- Shabua Days (page 153)

CHAPTER 4: THE SEVEN-DAY FEAST

THE SEVEN-DAY FEAST

BARLEY IS HARVESTED DURING NISAN: Look again at the discussion of the barley crop in Egypt and the plague of hail. What details from Exodus 9:31-32 accurately reflect how the crops mentioned actually grow—and why is the Bible's accuracy in such details important?

FEAST OF PASSOVER = FEAST OF UNLEAVENED BREAD: One feast has three names. List those names and also identify the precedent, the pattern, and the New Testament fulfillment associated with this feast.

NISAN 14: THE FIRST DATE OF THE SEVEN-DAY FEAST: What two requirements are associated with Nisan 14, the first date of the Seven-Day Feast?

NISAN 20: THE LAST DATE OF THE SEVEN-DAY FEAST: Explain how a Hebrew would understand "the twenty-first day of the month at evening" and therefore what the seven days of the Seven-Day Feast are.

> *Since we know the feast begins on Nisan 14 and lasts seven days, it must end on Nisan 20.*

NISAN 14 AND NISAN 20 ARE HOLY DAYS OF ASSEMBLY: How are holy days of assembly and days of solemn rest different?

7 NISAN 14: THE DATE THE PASSOVER LAMBS WERE KILLED: On what day was Jesus crucified? Why is that day significant? (Think precedent and pattern.)

JESUS WAS BURIED ON THE DAY OF PREPARATION: Why did the soldiers break the criminals' legs but not Jesus' legs? Address the physiology as well as the timing.

7 SEQUENCE OF EVENTS ON THE DAY OF PREPARATION: Look again at Figure 4.10. What had you never known before, what stood out to you, and/or what surprised you when you saw the way the events unfolded?

S LAMBS WERE SACRIFICED AT 9:00 A.M. AND 3:00 P.M.: Explain the significance of Jesus being crucified at 9:00 a.m. and dying at 3:00 p.m. (Again, think precedent and pattern.)

NISAN 15: THE DATE THE PASSOVER LAMBS WERE EATEN: What landmark event at the time of the exodus does the Passover meal commemorate?

THE PASSOVER SEDER INCLUDES FIFTEEN RITUALS: A little research will reveal the symbolism of many aspects of these rituals. Consider learning about the salt water, the broken matzah, the bitter vegetable, the charoset, and the closing cry "Next year in Jerusalem!" Have you ever participated in a Passover Seder? What significance, if any, did it hold for you?

S JESUS USED THE MOTZI BLESSING: Why is it significant that the Bible doesn't indicate that all fifteen parts of the Passover Seder rituals were performed at Jesus' Last Supper?

7 THE LAST SUPPER WAS NOT THE PASSOVER SEDER: (Yes, this section title is the answer to the preceding question.) Of the ten reasons why Jesus' Last Supper meal could not have been the Passover Seder, which reason(s) do you find most compelling? Why?

The day of Preparation meal that Jesus ate with His twelve disciples on Nisan 14 is typically referred to as the Lord's Supper or the Last Supper... The Last Supper meal on Nisan 14 could not have been the ceremonial Passover Seder observed on Nisan 15.

SEVEN DAYS IN EVERY SHABUA: Why are we referring to Saturday as the regular Sabbath?

It is important to understand that the Bible uses days as well as dates to specify exactly when biblical feasts, festivals, and holy days are to be celebrated... day will be used when referring to a specific day of the shabua, and date will be used when referring to a specific date of the month.

THE DISTINCTION BETWEEN A DAY AND A DATE: What aspect of Figure 4.15 did you find most helpful or interesting? Why? Also, what do you appreciate about the recurrence of precedent/pattern/prophecy?

NISAN 15 IS ALWAYS THE SABBATH HIGH DAY: Why didn't the Pharisees enter the headquarters of the Roman Governor Pontius Pilate? Why is this information key to determining what day Jesus and His disciples shared the Last Supper?

THAT SABBATH WAS A HIGH DAY: What does John emphasize about the day that followed the day of Preparation when Jesus was crucified?

S THE REGULAR SABBATH DURING THE SEVEN-DAY FEAST: Why do faithful Jews need to know when the regular Sabbath falls within the Seven-Day Feast?

THE REGULAR SABBATH VS. THE SABBATH HIGH DAY: Why do the regular Sabbath and the Sabbath High Day coincide every once in a while?

THE REGULAR SABBATH IN THE YEAR OF THE CRUCIFIXION: According to Luke, what happened on Nisan 14, Nisan 15, and Nisan16 in the year Jesus died?

DESIGNATED DAY WITHIN A FINITE RANGE OF DATES: What unique situation arises when Nisan 14 falls on a Thursday? on a Friday? What command about work did God give for those years when the day of Preparation (Nisan 14) falls on the regular Sabbath day of rest?

Designating a particular day instead of a date to celebrate holy days is still quite common today… examples include Thanksgiving Day (which is always celebrated on a Thursday) and Election Day (which always takes place on a Tuesday).

THE DAY AFTER THE SABBATH

THE BARLEY AND THE WHEAT HARVEST CEREMONIES: The timing of the two Old Testament spring feasts (pattern) is identical to the timing of the two New Testament spring feasts (prophecy). How is each of those dates determined?

DATES FOR THE BARLEY SHEAF FIRSTFRUITS CEREMONY: Why does the date of the regular Sabbath impact the day the general barley harvest could begin?

SYMBOLISM IN THE BARLEY SHEAF FIRSTFRUITS CEREMONY: In what ways are precedent, pattern, and prophecy evident in the symbolism of the barley sheaf firstfruits ceremony (Figure 4.19)?

7 THE RESURRECTION AND THE BARLEY FIRSTFRUITS SHEAF: Why is the resurrection of Jesus the foundation of a believer's faith? What commentary on Jesus' reputation as a great teacher does His resurrection offer?

7 THE SIGNIFICANCE OF THE RESURRECTION: Why does the resurrection validate Jesus' claims about His identity as well as everything else He said during His three-year ministry on this earth?

JESUS WAS RESURRECTED ON SUNDAY: What phrases in the words of the gospel writers (Figure 4.20) confirm that Jesus rose on Sunday?

Although the Bible does not specify exactly when it happened, it does indicate that Jesus was resurrected sometime during the first half of Sunday.

THE FIRST HALF OF SUNDAY, THE THIRD DAY: When did people begin to arrive at the empty tomb on Sunday? And when had Sunday begun?

S THREE DAYS AND THREE NIGHTS IN THE TOMB: Why is the phrasing "three days and three nights" odd for a Jew? Why did Jesus choose this wording?

The Bible does not specify either the day of the crucifixion or the date of the resurrection.

THE DAY AND DATE OF THE CRUCIFIXION AND RESURRECTION: Which conclusions in this section and in Figure 4.22 might people (and maybe you're one of them) push back against? What would be a helpful response?

S EIGHT LANDMARK DAYS AND DATES INVOLVING JESUS: Take the time to study and comprehend Figure 4.10, Figure 4.16, Figure 4.22, and Figure 4.23. After thoroughly looking over all of these schedules, will you think of Palm Sunday, Good Friday, and Easter Sunday any differently? Are there any changes you will make in the way you celebrate them? If so, what?

SHABUA-DAYS IN PRECEDENT, PATTERN, AND PROPHECY: What have you found most striking about the correlation of the *shabua*-days of the exodus (precedent), the *shabua*-days of the Seven-Day Feast (pattern), and the *shabua*-days of Jesus in the first century CE (prophecy)?

Write or list one or two takeaways from chapter 4 that you found most eye-opening, helpful, and/or intriguing.

I Want to Remember

I Have a Few Questions

SESSION 7

Pages 171-203 in *Shabua Days*

The Bible states that the Feast of Shabua is to be celebrated on a particular day, not a particular date. That day is Sunday; technically speaking, the day after the seventh regular Sabbath.

- Shabua Days (page 178)

CHAPTER 5: THE FEAST OF SHABUA

S A COMMEMORATION AND A FORESHADOWING: Are you convinced that the consistent and repeated use of Bible precedent, pattern, and prophecy makes a compelling case that the symmetry is by design and not merely a coincidence? Why or why not?

S THE FEAST OF SHABUA IS ON THE DAY OF PENTECOST: Both the Feast of *Shabua* and Pentecost mark the birth of something significant. What is remembered and celebrated on those two occasions?

S ISRAEL AND BELIEVERS ARE AS FIRSTFRUITS TO THE LORD: The two loaves of bread represent two people groups. Who are the people groups, and, in regard to those groups, what is significant about the leaven in the bread?

FEAST OF SHABUA TIMING

THE DAY TO CELEBRATE THE FEAST OF SHABUA: When initially looking over all of the Scriptures in Figure 5.1 there may seem to be discrepancies in when the Bible says the Feast of *Shabua* is to be celebrated. Explain in your own words why this is not true.

THE REGULAR SABBATH DURING THE SEVEN-DAY FEAST: Why is the day after every regular Sabbath always Sunday?

Shabua-days govern short-term timing in the Bible. It is a complete time period of seven days that includes six days of work or activity followed by a 7th and final day of rest. Shabua-days begin on Sunday and end on the regular Sabbath.

SEVEN WEEKS AND 7 SHABUA-DAYS: Name two similarities and one difference between one week and one *shabua*-days.

THE DAY AFTER 7 SHABUA-DAYS: Why is the Sunday following 7 *shabua*-days appropriately called Pentecost?

Thanksgiving in America is always celebrated on a particular day. That day is Thursday; technically speaking, the fourth Thursday in the month of November. If Thanksgiving were improperly linked to a date (such as November 25), the day would incorrectly vary from year to year.

THE FEAST OF SHABUA ALWAYS OCCURS ON SUNDAY: Explain the analogy between the date of America's Thanksgiving and the date of Israel's Feast of *Shabua*.

NO ORDINARY WORK ON DAY OF HOLY CONVOCATION: Why did the general wheat harvest always begin on Monday?

7 DATES FOR THE FEAST OF SHABUA: Why is a list of possible Sabbath days needed to determine the Feast of *Shabua*? Why do the dates of the Sabbath start with Nisan 14? Look at pages 138-139 in *Shabua Days*.

TWO SUNDAYS 7 SHABUA-DAYS APART: Why does determining the timing of the Feast of *Shabua* require the 7 *shabua*-days to begin the day after the regular Sabbath, which is always Sunday?

S THE COUNTING OF THE OMER: What parallel dating is reasonably assumed based on the consistent, predictable, and reliable use of timing in Bible precedent, pattern, and prophecy?

OVERVIEW OF THE FEAST OF SHABUA: Explain the interconnectedness of a landmark Old Testament event, the Feast of *Shabua*, and a landmark New Testament event.

CREATING A BIBLE CALENDAR

MANNA IN THE MORNING ON IYAR 15: In what way did God's gift of manna reflect the *shabua*-days pattern?

DATING THE FIRST SHABUA-DAYS OF MANNA: What detail in Exodus 16:1 is key to dating the first *shabua*-days of manna?

THREE MONTHS IN THE YEAR OF THE EXODUS: According to Exodus 16:1, manna appeared for the first time on the morning of Iyar 15. What about the account of that first week of manna (Exodus 16:21-26) enables us to determine that Iyar 15 was Sunday?

7 OBSERVATIONS BASED ON FIGURE 5.6: Sometimes the Bible states the DAY something happened but not the DATE. In those cases, how are DATES for biblical events determined?

The exodus and the crucifixion are linked through precedent, pattern, and prophecy. The symmetry between these two events is so detailed, specific, and comprehensive that coincidence can virtually be ruled out.

THE EXODUS AND THE CRUCIFIXION ARE LINKED: What source was used to determine the DAYS and DATES for events of the exodus and the crucifixion? What additional disciplines will provide further support in *Shabua Seventy*?

Every biblical month begins with the first visible sighting of the new moon immediately after sunset, an event referred to as Rosh Chodesh (the first or head of the month).

SIX DAYS AT MOUNT SINAI

ON THE DAY OF THE THIRD NEW MOON: What was the date of the third new moon—and what happened on that day?

SIVAN 1 THROUGH SIVAN 6: Why do we know that Sivan 6 was a Sunday? Figure 5.6 will help.

THE CHRONOLOGY OF THE FIRST SIX DAYS OF SIVAN: What fact(s) about the setting and the number of people, if any, surprised you?

TUESDAY, SIVAN 1: What signaled the beginning of a new day for the children of Israel? Of a new month? What four parts of every 24-hour period did Bible writers often use?

WEDNESDAY, SIVAN 2: What did Moses do on Sivan 2?

THURSDAY, SIVAN 3: What message did Moses have for the Lord on Sivan 3?

FRIDAY, SIVAN 4 ("TODAY"): After ascending Mount Sinai a second time, what did Moses do per the Lord's instruction? Why was this necessary? See Exodus 19:10-11.

REGULAR SABBATH, SIVAN 5 ("TOMORROW"): Per the Lord's instruction in Exodus 19:10-11, what happened on Sivan 5?

SUNDAY, SIVAN 6 ("THE THIRD DAY"): What happened in the morning of Sivan 6? What natural phenomena marked this event?

7 MIRACLES DURING THE EXODUS FROM EGYPT: Imagine witnessing any one of these miracles. How might it have impacted you and your belief that there is/isn't a God? How long might any one of these experiences impact your faith and trust? From what you know, does one miracle—or even a series of miracles—secure a person's faith for good? Why/why not?

THUNDER, LIGHTNING, FIRE, SMOKE, AND TREMBLING: Why does it seem appropriate for God to descend in fire and answer in thunder?

On Sunday, Sivan 6, after Moses brought the people out of the camp to the foot of Mount Sinai, Moses spoke to God, and God answered him in thunder.

THE TEN COMMANDMENTS

S GOD GAVE ISRAEL THE TEN COMMANDMENTS: In what ways did God demonstrate His power over Egyptian gods, idols, and even nature itself? Be specific. And in what ways have the Ten Commandments shaped not only the nation of Israel but people around the world for thousands of years?

THREE OBLIGATIONS IN THE TEN COMMANDMENTS: List the three kinds of obligations found in the Ten Commandments.

TWO TABLETS OF STONE WRITTEN BY GOD: What happened to the two tablets of stone God had written the commandments on? (What impact had all those miracles during the exodus had on the people of Israel and their faith in God?)

> *The replacement set of the two stone tablets was kept in a sacred gold chest called the Ark of the Covenant... When King Solomon built the First Temple in Jerusalem, the Ark containing the two tablets engraved with the Ten Commandments was set on the foundation stone within the temple's Most Holy Place (also called the Holy of Holies).*

7 JESUS DID NOT ABOLISH THE TEN COMMANDMENTS: Jesus came to fulfill the Old Testament law, and often that fulfillment involved expanding the reach of the law. For instance, how did Jesus broaden the application of "You shall not murder" in Matthew 3:21-22?

7 THE CHURCH AND THE SABBATH: Only one command is not repeated in the New Testament, nor is it applied to the church. In what way does Jesus fulfill the promise and possibility of rest? See Matthew 11:28.

JESUS LEFT OUT THE SABBATH OBLIGATION: What did Jesus teach are the two most important commands?

A SABBATH REST REMAINS FOR ISRAEL: What does the phrase "my rest" refer to? What second kind of rest can the people of Israel choose?

I Want to Remember

I Have a Few Questions

SESSION 8

Pages 203-218 in *Shabua Days*

The meticulous attention to detail coupled with unparalleled accuracy creates a compelling case that the precedents, patterns, and prophecies are in fact God breathed and true.

- Shabua Days (page 203)

CHAPTER 5: THE FEAST OF SHABUA

PRECEDENT, PATTERN, AND PROPHECY

7 MOUNT SINAI, THE FEAST OF SHABUA, AND PENTECOST: What did God's people receive at Mount Sinai (precedent)? What did Jesus' followers receive on Pentecost (prophecy fulfilled)? What connection does the Feast of *Shabua* have with both events (pattern)?

ON THE 50TH DAY: In addition to happening on the same day and date, what do the events of Mount Sinai and Pentecost have in common—and what does its appearance signify?

S TWO TABLETS, TWO LOAVES, TWO SIDES OF THE HEART: Trace the theme of sin through the Ten Commandments, the two loaves of bread, and the truth of Acts 2:21.

The gospel is not etched on two stone tablets or represented in two loaves of bread. The gospel is written on tablets (plural) of the human heart. It is noteworthy that, like the two stone tablets and the two loaves of bread, the human heart has two distinct sides. The heart has a thick wall of muscle—called the septum—that separates the chamber on the right side from the chamber on the left side.

7 ISRAEL AND THE CHURCH ARE BOTH FIRSTFRUITS: The Feast of *Shabua*'s wheat loaves ceremony featured a commemorative loaf and a prophetic loaf. What was being commemorated, and what future event was being acknowledged? Why are both Israel and the church firstfruits?

THE ROCK, A MASS OF ROCK, A STONE, A PIECE OF ROCK, LIVING STONES: What was foreshadowed in Jesus being the Rock that provided for the people of Israel in the wilderness?... In what ways is Jesus the rock-solid foundation for the church?... What is appropriate about both names—Simon and Peter—as well as when Jesus used each?... Jesus is the Rock. Peter's new name meant he was a piece of the Rock. What does it mean that New Testament believers are "living stones" (1 Peter 2:5-6)?

THE ROCK WAS STRUCK ONE TIME AND WATER CAME OUT: What did the water at Rephidim and the water from Jesus' side symbolize?

TALK TO THE ROCK AFTER IT HAD BEEN STRUCK ONE TIME: Jesus was struck on Calvary: He suffered and died on the cross. Now what are His followers to speak?

LIFE-SUSTAINING WATER PROVIDED BY THE ROCK: Compare the water that flowed at both Rephidim and Kadesh with the water that Jesus offers even today.

7 THE LAST DAY AND DATE WITH THE ROCK: What is significant about Iyar 26 during the exodus and after Jesus rose from the grave?

S GOD APPEARED TEN DAYS AFTER THURSDAY, IYAR 26: Describe God's appearance to the people of Israel ten days after Thursday, Iyar 26. Then describe how He made His presence known ten days after Thursday, Iyar 26, in the New Testament.

S TWO HOLY DAYS BEFORE GOD APPEARED ON SUNDAY: What happened in the two consecutive holy days during the exodus? What two consecutive holy days preceded Jesus' resurrection from the grave?

GOD CAME DOWN FROM HEAVEN MANIFEST AS FIRE: Comment on why fire is an appropriate symbol of God as well as an appropriate manifestation of His presence.

GOD SPOKE TO THE PEOPLE AND THROUGH THE APOSTLES: What is significant about the fact that God speaks through His people today just as He spoke through the apostles on Pentecost?

> *On the day that the apostles preached the gospel in Jerusalem, about 3,000 people were saved by grace from the consequences of their sin.*

3,000 DIED UNDER THE LAW; 3,000 WERE SAVED BY GRACE: What gospel truth is illustrated by this Old Testament/New Testament contrast? See John 3:16.

7 MOUNT SINAI, THE FEAST OF SHABUA, AND PENTECOST: The landmark Old Testament event at Mount Sinai (precedent), the annual commemorative Old Testament Feast of *Shabua* (pattern), and the foreshadowed New Testament event in Jerusalem on the day of Pentecost (prophecy) are all linked by subject matter as well as by timing. What is the subject matter that connects Mount Sinai and Pentecost? What do you find striking about the timing?

7 THE SIGNIFICANCE OF UNDERSTANDING SHABUA: Why is an understanding of *shabua* key to understanding the timing of events in the Old Testament? What advantages come with seeing the interrelationship between the exodus, biblical feasts, Jesus, the church, and the Bible's description of end times?

All Old Testament feasts, festivals, and holy days foreshadow New Testament events in a similar manner.

S SHABUA YEARS, THE SEQUEL: What do you find most intriguing in this preview of what *Shabua Years* will cover?

Write or list one or two takeaways from chapter 5 that you found most eye-opening, helpful, and/or intriguing.

For more information on [each of the three primary Old Testament biblical feasts], read the books of Exodus, Leviticus, Numbers, Deuteronomy, and the Gospels. There you will see the way multiple Old Testament precedents and patterns are linked to prophecies fulfilled in the New Testament.

I Want to Remember

I Have a Few Questions

LEADERS GUIDE

Thank you for your commitment to leading a group through *Shabua Days*. You have chosen an important role and will soon find that you will be greatly rewarded for it. We hope that as you lead, your knowledge and understanding of Scripture and your faith in Jesus will greatly increase.

Throughout the study your group will review questions that encourage thought-provoking group discussions. Your role as the group leader is to guide the discussion so that everyone has time to process, question, and reflect upon what they read in *Shabua Days*.

This study guide was designed to be read in tandem with the book *Shabua Days*. Therefore, we suggest that you encourage everyone to get their own copies of each. In addition, as the leader, we hope that you will encourage everyone to read the required material in *Shabua Days* and make use of the space provided in this study guide to write down any answers, notes, questions, and thoughts.

MEETINGS

Consider meeting weekly for sixty or ninety minutes. (As the group leader, it is up to you to keep track of time and keep things moving.) This study guide contains eight sessions that correspond with readings in *Shabua Days*. Since there is a lot of material that is covered in each session, you can move at a slower pace if you prefer, by dividing the longer chapters and increasing the number of times you meet.

The materials that you should recommend everyone to bring to each group meeting are:

- The book *Shabua Days*

- This study guide (*Shabua Days Study Guide*)

- Bible (either book or electronic)

- Something to write with

Before every meeting, we suggest you review the assigned questions. Even though there are a lot of questions in each session, don't feel like you have to go over all of them. Choose those questions that you find most worthwhile to camp on and discuss. Note which of those questions you absolutely don't want to miss. The icon **7** indicates questions you might consider. The icon **S** indicates questions you might look at if time allows.

We recommend that the small-group study time go something like this:

- Open with a time a prayer

- Have people share their "I Want to Remember" from the session you are reviewing (this will ease people into discussion as well as be a helpful review of some things that were covered)

- Discuss **7** questions

- Discuss **S** questions (if time allows)

- If any "I Have a Few Questions" are not answered during the discussion time then now would be the time to go over those

- Close with a time of prayer

STUDY GUIDE SESSION BREAKDOWN

- Session 1: *Shabua Days* pages 1-26
  (Chapter 1 through Chapter 2's "The Inaugural Shabua")

- Session 2: *Shabua Days* pages 26-56
  (Chapter 2's "The Big Bang's Universe" through "The Bible's Universe")

- Session 3: *Shabua Days* pages 57-87
  (Chapter 2's "Evolution's Diversity" through "The Bible vs. Secular Science")

- Session 4: *Shabua Days* pages 89-118
  (Chapter 3)

- Session 5: *Shabua Days* pages 119-136
  (Chapter 4 through "Marking Time in the Bible")

- Session 6: *Shabua Days* pages 136-170
  (Chapter 4's "The Seven-Day Feast" through "The Day After the Sabbath")

- Session 7: *Shabua Days* pages 171-203
  (Chapter 5 through "The Ten Commandments")

- Session 8: *Shabua Days* pages 203-218
  (Chapter 5's "Precedent, Pattern, and Prophecy")

DETAILED CONTENTS

(For *Shabua Days*)

CPSIA information can be obtained
at www.ICGtesting.com
Printed in the USA
FSHW010812050419